First World War
and Army of Occupation
War Diary
France, Belgium and Germany

34 DIVISION
Divisional Troops
175 Brigade Royal Field Artillery
30 August 1915 - 31 December 1916

WO95/2448/1

Published by

The Naval & Military Press Ltd

Unit 10 Ridgewood Industrial Park,

Uckfield, East Sussex,

TN22 5QE England

Tel: +44 (0) 1825 749494

www.naval-military-press.com

www.nmarchive.com

This diary has been reprinted in facsimile from the original. Any imperfections are inevitably reproduced and the quality may fall short of modern type and cartographic standards.

© **Crown Copyright**
Images reproduced by permission of The National Archives, London, England, 2015.

Contents

Document type	Place/Title	Date From	Date To
Heading	34th Division 175th Bde R.F.A. Jan-Dec 1916 To 1 Army		
Heading	175. Bde Rfa 34 Div Vol 1		
War Diary	Tidworth	30/08/1915	02/09/1915
War Diary	Corton	02/10/1915	10/01/1916
War Diary	Harve	11/01/1916	12/01/1916
War Diary	St Omer	11/01/1916	11/01/1916
War Diary	Wittes	23/01/1916	13/02/1916
War Diary	Armentieres	19/02/1916	30/04/1916
War Diary	Bayenghem Seninghem	01/05/1916	07/05/1916
War Diary	Albert	08/05/1916	30/06/1916
Heading	34th Div. III. Corps War Diary Headquarters, 175th Brigade, R.F.A. July 1916		
War Diary	Albert	01/07/1916	30/07/1916
War Diary	Albert	01/07/1916	06/07/1916
Heading	34th Divisional Artillery. 175th Brigade Royal Field Artillery August 1916		
Heading	War Diary Of 175th F A Brigade From 1st To 31st August 1916 Volume 8		
War Diary	Albert	01/08/1916	19/08/1916
War Diary	Behencourt	20/08/1916	21/08/1916
War Diary	Les Haies Bsses	22/08/1916	24/08/1916
War Diary	Armentieres	25/08/1916	28/08/1916
Heading	War Diary Of 175th F.A Brigade From 1st To 30th Sept. 1916 Volume 9		
War Diary	Chapelle d'Armentieres	01/09/1916	22/09/1916
War Diary	Armentieres	22/09/1916	30/09/1916
Heading	War Diary Of 175th Brigade R.F.A. From 1st to 31st Oct. 1916 Volume 10		
War Diary	Armentieres	01/10/1916	31/10/1916
Heading	War Diary of 175th Brigade R.F.A. From 1st to 30th Nov 1916 Volume 10		
War Diary	Armentieres	03/11/1916	29/11/1916
Heading	War Diary of 175th Brigade R.F.A. From 1st to 31st Dec 1916 Volume XI		
War Diary	Armentieres	02/12/1916	11/12/1916
War Diary	Armentieres	10/12/1916	31/12/1916

34TH DIVISION

175TH BDE R.F.A.

JAN - DEC 1916

TO 1 ARMY

175. Bde
R7.a.
34Dw
Vol I

Jan '16
Dec '16

Army Form C. 2118.

WAR DIARY
or
INTELLIGENCE SUMMARY.
(Erase heading not required.)

175th Staffordshire Brigade R.F.A.

Instructions regarding War Diaries and Intelligence Summaries are contained in F.S. Regs., Part II. and the Staff Manual respectively. Title pages will be prepared in manuscript.

Place	Date	Hour	Summary of Events and Information	Remarks and references to Appendices
Tidworth	30 Aug		The Brigade was locally raised in Staffordshire by Lt Col S.C. Impey Thomas B.F.A. M.P. Recruiting commenced 25th June 1915 and closed approximately on the 12th August 1915 when the Brigade joined the 34th Division and moved to Kirby Mulgrave. Division moved to Tidworth	E.S.C. Impey Lt Col
"	2 Sept		Lt Col S.H. Stevenson D.S.O. R.F.A. assumes command of the Brigade	
Cocton	2 Oct		Brigade moves to Cocton to complete training	
"			Brigade warned for service in Egypt (middle December) cancelled a week later	
"	3 Jan 16		Again warned this time for service in France.	
"	10 pm		Entrained for France. Sailed same night from Southampton for Havre	
Havre	11 Jan		Arrived Havre after uneventful passage.	
"	11 & 12 Jan		Entrained for St Omer. 12 & 13 Jan arrived safely and marched into Billets	
St Omer			A,B,C, Btys at Celly HQ, D Bty " Arqueles a.c. " Ingham	
Wittes	23		34th Division is attached to 3rd Corps, 1st Army. Brigade moves into billets at Wittes.	E.S.C. Impey Lt Col

Army Form C. 2118.

WAR DIARY
or
INTELLIGENCE SUMMARY.
(Erase heading not required.)

Place	Date	Hour	Summary of Events and Information	Remarks and references to Appendices
Witts	25 Jan		Orders received that 34th Division is to relieve 23rd Division in action at Armentières, 175th Brigade to relieve 104th RFA 13th. Parties of officers and men sent up to Armentières to visit positions	E.V.[signature]

Army Form C. 2118.

WAR DIARY
or
INTELLIGENCE SUMMARY.
(Erase heading not required.)

175th Staffs F.A. Bde.

Instructions regarding War Diaries and Intelligence Summaries are contained in F.S. Regs., Part II. and the Staff Manual respectively. Title pages will be prepared in manuscript.

Place	Date	Hour	Summary of Events and Information	Remarks and references to Appendices
Wilkes	9th Feb		One section from each battery leaves for the front to start relief of 104th Bde. They take over that night.	
"	11th		Headquarters move to Armentières	
"	13th		Second section from each battery moves up. Total relief of all batteries completed. 104th Bde Battery Commanders however still in charge. 175th Bde takes over 104th Bde's guns which are left in position.	
Armentières	12th	12 noon	104th Bde Headquarters leave. 175th Bde takes over.	
"	13		Our first casualties. 3 men of D'Battery killed by the bursting of the gun they were serving. "C" Battery's OP at Ferme du Bies demolished by shell fire.	
"	14/15		"D" Battery's OP at Lille Post also demolished by shell fire.	
"	16		Very quiet. Bde is the left flank Bde of 1st Army. On our right are the 160th FA Bde of which 2 batteries "C" and "D" are attached to us forming the left FA group commanded by Lt Col E.H. Stevenson DSO RFA; Affiliated to this group is the Warwick battery (Heavier 4.7) and "E" Battery 176th FA Bde (H.E. Hows). On our left is the 96th F.A. Bde. 21st Div.	

2353 Wt W2544/1454 700,000 5/15 D, D, & L. A.D.S.S./Forms/C. 2118.

WAR DIARY
or
INTELLIGENCE SUMMARY

Army Form C. 2118.

Vol 2

175 Bde (less) R.F.A.

Place	Date	Hour	Summary of Events and Information	Remarks and references to Appendices
Armentières	1-5 March		quiet	
	6	2.30 p.m.	A and D Batteries took part in a small scheme shelling trenches with satisfactory results	
	7		quiet	
	8		B. Battery shelled trenches effectively	
	9-12		quiet	
	13		Small scheme to cut wire and breach parapet successfully carried out	
	14-25		quiet	
	26		B&D "B"/175 in farm house close to position shelled and set on fire. A few casualties were sustained by this battery during the night when enemy again opened and shrapnel	
	28-29		quiet	
	22		The Brigade join 2nd Army but remain in same position. The 2 Batteries "C" & "D" of the 160 Bde leave our group to join their own brigade.	
	25-27		in position further south. "C" Battery 176 Bde (How) R.F.A. joins group. Left group now consists of A B C & D 18 Bdg. 175 F.A. Bde. "C" Bdy 176 F.A (How) and "C" 85, 79 F.A. Bde. Which joined our group on the 27"	

Malcolm Fletcher
Lt Col RFA
comdg 175 Bde

XXXIV
175th Bde R.F.A. Vol 3

Army Form C. 2118.

WAR DIARY
or
INTELLIGENCE SUMMARY.
(Erase heading not required.)

Instructions regarding War Diaries and Intelligence Summaries are contained in F. S. Regs., Part II. and the Staff Manual respectively. Title pages will be prepared in manuscript.

Place	Date	Hour	Summary of Events and Information	Remarks and references to Appendices
Armentières	April 1 to 10		Very quiet. News that we are to be relieved here by Australians. Australian 4th Bde of 2nd Div arrive. Their BCs HQ officers and about 60 men are attached to Btys. Relief started night of 9th	
	10 April 10am		Relief completed 4th Bde AFA takes charge. 175 FA Bde marches into billets at Witte	
	12th		We march into billets at Bayinghem (by Lumbres) and neighbouring villages	
	12 to 30th		Bde Training	

M Hamilton Fletcher
Lt Col
175 Bde R.F.A.

Army Form C. 2118.

VOL 4
XXIV 175 RFA

WAR DIARY
or
INTELLIGENCE SUMMARY.
(Erase heading not required.)

Instructions regarding War Diaries and Intelligence Summaries are contained in F.S. Regs., Part II. and the Staff Manual respectively. Title pages will be prepared in manuscript.

Place	Date	Hour	Summary of Events and Information	Remarks and references to Appendices
Bayenghem les Seninghem	May 1st to 4th 5th		Brigade still in training	
	5th		Brigade entrained at WIZERNES for forward area. Detrained at Longeau and marched to billets in BEHENCOURT. Rested at billets.	
	6th			
	7th			
Albert	8th		Marched to ALBERT	
	9th		On the night of 8th/9th one section A/175 relieved one section "D" By RHA	
	10th		On the night of 9th/10th one section B/175 relieved position formerly occupied employed	
	11th		On the night of 10th/11th one section C/175 relieved one section (detached) "D" By R.H.A.	
	12th		On the night of 11th/12th " " " B/175 " " " 1st By R.F.A.	
			" " " 11/12 " " " A/175 relieved remaining section "O" By R.H.A	
			" " " 11/12 " " " C/175 " " one section (detached)	
			This completed all reliefs.	
			The remaining battery D/176 carried on with the new position.	
			The Group consists of A, B, C, D By 175. C, D By 176, of which D/175 and D/176 are out of action, under Lt Col. E.H. Stevenson DSO RFA.	

Army Form C. 2118.

WAR DIARY
or
INTELLIGENCE SUMMARY.
(Erase heading not required.)

Place	Date	Hour	Summary of Events and Information	Remarks and references to Appendices
Albert	13th		Quiet	
	16, 21, M			
	22nd		The Howitzer Brigade was split up, one battery being posted to each 18pr Bde in the Group instead of one of the 18pr. Batteries. This necessitated a change in the denomination of batteries concerned. The following are the changes:—	
			C/175 becomes C/176	
			D/175 " C/175	
			D/176 " D/175	
			C/176 (now Group) becomes D/152.	
	23rd to 31st		Quiet	

J. R. Brindly, Colonel
for Commanding 175 Bde R.F.A.
+ Left Group of R.A.

WAR DIARY or INTELLIGENCE SUMMARY

Army Form C. 2118.

34 JUNE

175th Brigade Royal Field Artillery

Vol 5

Place	Date	Hour	Summary of Events and Information	Remarks and references to Appendices
ALBERT	1916 June 1.		The 175 B.ie. RFA. formed part of the I.O. or Left Group in action. A and B/175 RFA were in action 400 yards E. of ALBERT and 200 yards N. of the ALBERT — BAPAUME ROAD. C and D/175 RFA and C/176 RFA were in action near AUTHVILLE WOOD. The Above formed the I.O. Group	
	1 – 3		No important operations took place.	
	4 – 5		At about 1.0 A.M a heavy fire was opened by the enemy commenced on the right of the Group all Batteries prepared for action. Having heard that there was an enemy attack on the Right we co-operated with the Right Group by forming a barrage on the German trenches. For some time it was thought that the Germans were attacking our trenches also but this turned out to be wrong. At about 9.0 PM heavy shelling commenced again on our right and on our trenches about KEATS REDAN and DUNFERMLINE STREET. Our Batteries immediately opened fire on the enemy front line. On information from the Right Group I.O. Group again formed a barrage to support them. Communications were a difficulty.	
	5/6		At 11.0 PM. I.O. Group bombarded Southern outlying trenches of	

Army Form C. 2118.

WAR DIARY
or
INTELLIGENCE SUMMARY.
(Erase heading not required.)

Instructions regarding War Diaries and Intelligence Summaries are contained in F. S. Regs., Part II. and the Staff Manual respectively. Title pages will be prepared in manuscript.

Place	Date	Hour	Summary of Events and Information	Remarks and references to Appendices
ALBERT	1916 June 5/6		LA BOISELLE in Support of a raid by our Infantry. Fire was continued until 12.15 A.M. All was quiet again by 1.10 A.M. Communicators worked very well.	
	6/7		Quiet.	
	8		A, B and C/175 Bde RFA were relieved in action by 3 Batteries of the 176th Bde. RFA (Lt. Col. R.T. Rundle, CB, Com'dg). A, B & C/175 RFA moved into rest at their Wagon Lines.	
	12		A, B & C/175 RFA returned to their positions in action.	
	17		Col. Capt. Rundle, CB (15th over Command of the 1.0. Group consisting of 175th Bde complete with Staff and C/176 RFA.	
	11-17		Preliminary orders received daily and varied daily to Batteries for a Bombardment of the German Line in the Group Zone to commence at late date were received	
	22		Final orders for Preliminary Bombardment and for an attack on a future date on the German Line East of ALBERT. 2nd Lt. C. FREEMAN - COWAN was killed by a shell. He had just completed the 1.0 Group Telephone Comm'n System.	

Army Form C. 2118.

WAR DIARY
or
INTELLIGENCE SUMMARY.
(Erase heading not required.)

Place	Date	Hour	Summary of Events and Information	Remarks and references to Appendices
ALBERT	1916 June 24/30		I.O. Group carried out the Preliminary Bombardment, Rehearsal of lifts to take place on the day of attack, The BRITISH-FRENCH wire cutting, night Barrage of communications and the keeping open of wire cut in LABOISELLE and FRONT & SUPPORT & 2ND LINE TRENCHES. During these proceedings the enemy retaliation was very feeble. The wire cutting was very successfully carried out. According to statements by German deserters during this period the night Barrages on all roads and approaches were exceedingly satisfactory and considerably interfered with the German food supply. The Day of Assault was postponed from the 29th of June to the 1st of July.	
	30		Lt. Col. W. Fuminall. R.F.A. took over command of the I.O. Group at 9.0 A.M. in succession to Lt. Col. E.H. Stevenson, D.S.O, R.F.A. Commanding 175th Brigade R.F.A.	

W. Fuminall
Lt Col RFA

34th Div.
III.Corps.

WAR DIARY

Headquarters,

175th BRIGADE, R.F.A.

J U L Y

1 9 1 6

Volume 7.

Army Form C. 2118.

175th Brigade. R.F.A. Page 1.

Vol 6

WAR DIARY
or
INTELLIGENCE SUMMARY.
(Erase heading not required.)

Place	Date	Hour	Summary of Events and Information	Remarks and references to Appendices
ALBERT	1916 1st July	6.30 AM	Bombardment commenced.	
		7.30 AM	British Infantry crossed No Man's Land to the attack on the German positions East of ALBERT. The Brigade co-operated with the Grenade posts, its zone allotted to it being the whole of La Boiselle salient and a strip about 750 yards wide running from the salient in a N.E'ly direction. The Infantry attack was greatly heed up by Machine Guns which the Enemy brought up from deep Dug Outs a/c the Bombardment and on (instances of) Infantry having passed behind them and on to the Enemy Support-Line were cut off. Three of these Machine Guns and detachments were knocked out by our guns. The fight then resolved itself as far as we were concerned into a struggle for the position of the labyrinth of trenches in and around LA BOISELLE. This village did not entirely pass into our hands until the 5th of July when the 19th Division Infantry consolidated a line running round its Northern and Eastern outskirts. During this time our Batteries were chiefly employed in preventing fresh troops and supplies reinforcing the LA BOISELLE garrison from the direction of Villers and at night engaged the approach from the Pozieres direction. This, according to the accounts of prisoners taken, was carried out most successfully. Also during this period	Appendix I.
	5th July			

Army Form C. 2118.

175th Brigade RFA

Page 2

WAR DIARY or INTELLIGENCE SUMMARY.

(Erase heading not required.)

Place	Date	Hour	Summary of Events and Information	Remarks and references to Appendices
ALBERT	**1916** 5th July		Several parties of the enemy in the now shallow trenches were effectually fired on and considerable casualties were observed.	
	6th July	6 p.m.	The Brigade was relieved by the 89th Brigade R.F.A., 19th Divn. A/175 was replaced under the orders of O.C. 160th Brigade RFA and moved into the forward position. B/175 under the orders of O.C. 152nd Bde RFA without moving. C/175, C/176 and D/152 were formed into a Mobile Group under Lt. Col. W. Turnwall. Of these B and C/175 batteries went into rest at DERNANCOURT. During the operations on the 1st to 6th July the Brigade lost two of its Officers killed & two Junior Officers. 2nd Lt. W.C. HICKMAN, killed and 2nd Lt. T. CRUMBIE, wounded. Both these Officers were Liaison Officers, the former attached to the Right Attacking Battalion and the latter to the Left. These Officers were replaced by 2nd Lt. LAMISTRE and 2nd Lt. WEBBER, two other Officers joined the Brigade about the same time, 2nd Lt. TWYFORD posted to A/175; 2nd Lt. LEMON posted to A/175 and Lieut. Fiennes posted to C/175 (17-VII-16). 2nd Lt. H. WILSON-JONES was attached from the Divl. Trench Mortar Battery to B/175 RFA (9-VII-16).	
	7th July			

Army Form C. 2118.

WAR DIARY
or
INTELLIGENCE SUMMARY.
(Erase heading not required.)

175th Brigade RFA Page 3

Place	Date	Hour	Summary of Events and Information	Remarks and references to Appendices
ALBERT	1916 July 14		A/175 RFA relieved 4/77 [?]	
			The positions in the 4 Batteries of the Brigade were selected on the 10th Inst. by Lt Col N Turnbull RFA, on the Eastern side of the Sausage Valley 1500 yards SE. of LA BOISELLE.	
		10	A/175 and B/175 RFA commenced digging their gun-pits in these positions.	
	11		B/175 RFA relieved A/175 RFA in the forward position of the Right Group.	
	14		A/175 RFA occupied their gun pits on the E. of Sausage Valley and C/175 RFA	
	17		occupied the gun-pits of B/175 RFA in that place	
	18		C/175 RFA dug new gun-pits in this position and occupied same. B/175 RFA moved into those pits already constructed by them.	
	19		D/175 RFA (Howitzers) occupied the gun-pits they had built in this Brigade position.	
	20		This Brigade was attached to the 23rd Divisional Artillery and F.O.O.'s registered the German Dunster Line with observation from "No Mans Land"	
	24		Lt Disandrich to 10th over Temporary Command of B/175 RFA, vice Capt. C.E. Howard sick.	
	26		Two Batteries B/152 and D/152 took over the position of A/175 and D/175 respectively.	

2353 Wt. W2344/1454 700,000 5/15 D,D.& L. A.D.S.S./Forms/C. 2118.

Army Form C. 2118.

WAR DIARY
or
INTELLIGENCE SUMMARY.
(Erase heading not required.)

175th Brigade RFA Page 4

Place	Date	Hour	Summary of Events and Information	Remarks and references to Appendices
Albert	1916 July 26		D/175 RFA went into rest at their wagon lines. A/175 and D/175 RFA returned into action and B/152 RFA relieved C/175 RFA with	
	28		went into rest at its wagon line.	
	30		C, D and B/175 RFA were relieved by B/152, D/152 and B/160 RFA respectively and went into rest at their wagon lines.	
			The principle objectives of the 175th Brigade RFA during this month is the bombardment of the SWITCH LINE, S.W. of MARTINPUICH and the barraging of approaches to the same; and Barrage fire N.E. of POZIERES in support of the attack by the Australian Division on that place, and subsequent attacks to the N and N.E. of that place. This fire has been continually observed from our front trenches by the Reg'ts of the Brigade.	

N. Stanwell
Lt Col RFA
Cmdr 175th Brigade RFA

175th Brigade RFA

Army Form C. 2118.

WAR DIARY
or
INTELLIGENCE SUMMARY.

APPENDIX I, July, 1916.

Place	Date	Hour	Summary of Events and Information	Remarks and references to Appendices
ALBERT	1916 July 1-6		Great resistance in the clearing up of LA BOISELLE by the Infantry Bombers was given by this Brigade's firing on the trenches of LA BOISELLE uncaptured.	
	1-6		From the evening of the 1st July the 18 Pdr. Batteries were firing continuously a barrage for 72 hours after which Batteries were relieved from firing by two hours at a time, but the barrage was continued up to the time of relief by 89th Brigade R.F.A.	

D. Lt.Col.

34th Divisional Artillery.

175th BRIGADE

ROYAL FIELD ARTILLERY

AUGUST 1 9 1 6 :‡:

Vol 7

Confidential
War Diary
- of -
175th F. A. Brigade
From 1st to 31st August 1916.

Volume 8

WAR DIARY
INTELLIGENCE SUMMARY

175th Brigade. R.F.A.

Vol VIII

Army Form C. 2118.

Place	Date	Hour	Summary of Events and Information	Remarks and references to Appendices
Albert	1916. Aug. 1st		A/175 in action in Horse Shoe Ridge Position, Sausage Valley. Group consisted of A/175, B/160, B/152, D/152. Objectives the Switch Line Trench and communications back from that & around MARTIN PUICH.	
	4th		Anzac Corps attacked O.G.1 and O.G.2. Brigade cooperated with fire on frontline near the BAPAUME ROAD.	
	5th		A/175 relieved by B/175 - firing continued as from 1st to 4th inst.	
	6th		C/175 relieved B/152, D/175 relieved D/152 - Sausage Valley heavily shelled by enemy	
	9th		B/175 relieved B/160	
	10th		A/175 relieved B/176 in action. Batteries fired continuous barrage 6 hrs on and 6 hrs off until 9.30 pm 12th inst.	
	12th		9.30 pm. Special bombardment Switch Line lasting 5 mins. 13th in support of 4th Australian Division and 15th Division.	
	13th		34th Div. Arty. resumed command of this brigade. Barrage continuous all night and till 2 am 14th.	
	15.16.		Intermittent firing on Switch Line & back approach to Martinpuich.	
	17th		Lt Col Moss Blundell Comdg. 251 Bde RFA. inspected Valley position preparatory to taking over. Attack on Switch Line at 9.5 am. Continuous bombardment up to time brigade was relieved	

Army Form C. 2118.

WAR DIARY
INTELLIGENCE SUMMARY
17 Brigade. R.F.A.

(Erase heading not required.)

Instructions regarding War Diaries and Intelligence Summaries are contained in F.S. Regs., Part II. and the Staff Manual respectively. Title pages will be prepared in manuscript.

Place	Date	Hour	Summary of Events and Information	Remarks and references to Appendices
Albert	Aug 1916. 10-			
	19.		One section ffa½ battery relieved by a section of 251. Brigade R.F.A. batteries — Relieved sections of Indian howitzer batteries at BEHENCOURT — receiving sections returned — Command of I.O. Group handed over by Lt Col W. Furnivall to Lt Col Moo Blundell at 6 p.m.	
BEHENCOURT	20.		Remaining sections returned. marched to BEHENCOURT — also Brigade Head quarters.	
	21		Brigade marched SALEUX via AMIENS and entrained	
LES HAIES BASSES	22nd 23rd		Brigade detrained at STEINBECQUE and marched to LES HAIES BASSES W.Bivouacked	
	24.		Brigade remained at LES HAIES BASSES. Sections took over two sections of 82nd Brigade R.F.A. in action BOIS GRENIER Front.	
ARMENTIÈRES	25.		Remaining sections in action — Lt Col W. Furnivall took over command in the line from Lt Col W. Thorp. Command 82nd Brigade R.F.A. Battery registered.	
	26-27.			
	28.		34th Aust Artillery front divided into two groups at 12 noon — at this time also the new organisation of two 6 gun 18/pr batteries & 1. 4.gun Howitzer Battery started B/17 was split up between A/17 and C/17. C/17 was renamed B/17.	N.Furnivall/Lt Col. Commd/17. Bde RFA

2353 Wt. W2544/1454 700,000 5/15 D.D.&L. A.D.S.S./Forms/C. 2118.

VOL 8

Confidential
War Diary
- of -
175th F.A. Brigade
From 1st to 30th Sept. 1916

Volume 9

Army Form C. 2118.

WAR DIARY
or
INTELLIGENCE SUMMARY.
(Erase heading not required.)

Volume 9

Instructions regarding War Diaries and Intelligence Summaries are contained in F. S. Regs., Part II and the Staff Manual respectively. Title pages will be prepared in manuscript.

Place	Date	Hour	Summary of Events and Information	Remarks and references to Appendices
CHAPELLE D'ARMENTIÈRES	SEPTEMBER 1916 1-20		A/175 RFA under command of The Right Group Commander, 34th Divisional Artillery.	
	21		B/175 & D/175 " " left " "	
			The 175th Brigade RFA withdrew from the Line and proceeded to the Wagon Lines near CROIX DU BAC	
	22	6.0 a.m.	The 175th Brigade RFA came under command of C.R.A. FRANKS' FORCE. Lt. Col. W. Furnivall in command of Right Group, Artillery, Franks Force. Right Group consisted of the 175th Brigade, A/152 R.F.A. and Y/34 Medium Trench Mortar Battery of own Battery.	
ARMENTIÈRES	22/23		One section of the Right Group, Franks Force relieved one section of the Right Group of the 51st (Highland) Divisional Artillery in position on the Eastern outskirts of ARMENTIÈRES and NOUVEL HOUPLINES	
	23/24		Remaining sections of the 51st Div. Arty. relieved by remaining sections of Right Group Battery, Franks Force.	
	24	11 a.m.	Lt. Col. W. Furnivall took over Group Control from Lt. Col. Dunrun A.F.A.T. The Batteries registered their Zero Lines.	
	25-27		Registration of Enemy Front Line Trenches, Communication Trenches and Junctions of Trenches carried out.	
			— Continued —	

Army Form C. 2118.

WAR DIARY
or
INTELLIGENCE SUMMARY.
(Erase heading not required.)

Instructions regarding War Diaries and Intelligence Summaries are contained in F.S. Regs., Part II. and the Staff Manual respectively. Title pages will be prepared in manuscript.

Volume 9

Place	Date	Hour	Summary of Events and Information	Remarks and references to Appendices
ARMENTIERES	SEPTEMBER 1916 28	1 P.M.	A scheme for the bombardment of the Railways Salient and enemy communication trenches in the vicinity was carried out. The 2" T.M. fired on the screen in Rahrm Salient and bombarded Parapets in front. The 4.5" Howitzers with 3" T.M.'s supped on the chord line of the salient and the 18 Pdrs on communication trenches.	
		10.10 P.M.	Above artillery strafe carried out with good considerable effect as the enemy were very active in replying. The enemy approximately fired bombardment strapnel/expended by 4.5 How 60 Rounds, by 18 Pdrs 180 Rounds, by 2" T.M.'s 20 Rounds, and by 3" T.M. 100 Rounds.	
	30	10.0 P.M. 6 P 10.30 P.M.	Co-operation with 34th Divisional Artillery for the purpose of covering 34th Division's Infantry raids. Right Group Artillery's objective was on the southern side of the Mushroom Salient to prevent Machine Gun fire enfilading No Man's Land. The firing was effective and the Raids successfully carried out without casualties. One prisoner was taken and two correct identifications obtained.	

R. Thurmond Lt. Col.
Comdg. 175 Brigade RFA

Vol 9

Confidential

War Diary

— of —

175th Brigade R.F.A.

From 1st to 31st Octr. 1916.

Volume 10.

WAR DIARY
INTELLIGENCE SUMMARY

Army Form C. 2118.

175th (Staff(s)) Brigade
Royal Field Artillery

Place	Date	Hour	Summary of Events and Information	Remarks and references to Appendices
ARMENTIERES	1st/10/16			
"	2/10/16 to 6/10/16		A scheme for a Raid on Enemy's Front line at Railway was arranged at H.Q., Franks Force to take place on the 6th. Batteries and Y/34 MTMB carried out wire cutting at 2 places opposite "Railway Salient" and 2 other Enemy places north and South of it. On the 3rd & 6th Newton Trench mortars were got into position in our front opposite the Railway Salient. These mortars co-operated in the Artillery scheme for this Raid being the first occasion these mortars has ever been used on the British front.	
"	7/10/16 1.25am		A party of 30 of 103 Infantry Brigade raided the "Railway Salient". No prisoners were made. Our Infantry suffered no casualties and pronounced artillery bombardment and barrage excellent. No Difficulty was experienced with wire. On this day another scheme was arranged at G.O.C. Franks Force H.Q. for a raid on a larger scale to take place on the 12th inst. The Chemin lui of the Railway Salient being the objective. The 516th How Battery T.F. ~~~~~ joined the brigade on this day and became "E" Bty 175 Bde R.F.A., remaining at it's wagon lines.	cont

WAR DIARY or INTELLIGENCE SUMMARY.

Army Form C. 2118.

(Erase heading not required.)

Place	Date	Hour	Summary of Events and Information	Remarks and references to Appendices
ARMENITIERES	8/10/16 to 11/10/16		Batteries and M.T.M Bty carried out wire-cutting at various points on the enemy's front and a bombardment by Howitzers of objective for scheme.	
	12/10/16	5.30pm	A party of 100 men of the 103 Infantry Bde raided the enemy's chord line of "Railway Salient". The wire were found to be completely cut by our artillery and the trenches much damaged. The infantry again barraged Barrage and artillery fire which lasted for 1 hour 5 mins excellent. Several of the enemy were killed by our infantry but no prisoners were attained. Lieut Colonel W Furnivall proceeded on ten days leave to England and handed over command of Right group Franks Force to Captain R.W. Ardagh 175 Brigade R.F.A.	
	14/10/16		Our Artillery was active in retaliation to enemy's fire. Several targets were registered by batteries with aeroplane observation.	
	14/10/16 and 15/10/16			
	16/10/16		D/175 heavily shelled two houses used as a "strong point" and an a 3 inch. O.P. many direct hits were attained.	
	17/10/16		According to a scheme arranged Right group bombarded enemy's works and carried out a dummy raid with fire.	

Cont.

Army Form C. 2118.

WAR DIARY
or
INTELLIGENCE SUMMARY.
(Erase heading not required.)

(Cont)

Instructions regarding War Diaries and Intelligence Summaries are contained in F.S. Regs., Part II and the Staff Manual respectively. Title pages will be prepared in manuscript.

Place	Date	Hour	Summary of Events and Information	Remarks and references to Appendices
ARMENTIERES	18/10/16		Orders were received for a Raid by the 103 Infantry Brigade on the "Sparrow's Nest". Wire cutting was commenced at several places	
"	19/10/16		Wire cutting and registration for scheme was continued.	
"	20/10/16	12.00p	Right group fired for raid for 45 mins. Our infantry had no casualties. Barrage and bombardment was very effective. Raid was unsuccessful. The wire was not well cut.	
"	21/10/16		D/175 fired with observation from Sound Ranging Section. This officer reported that the Sound Ranging Section could tell exactly when each round fell.	
"	23/10/16		Right Battery carried out Bombardment to damage enemy works and to inflict casualties.	
"	25/10/16		Registration with aeroplane observation carried out.	
"	26/10/16		Right group carried out S.O.S. barrage, 280 Rounds being fired.	
"	29/10/16		S.O.S. barrage was again fired, 680 Rounds were fired.	
"	30/10/16	6.30 a	15 min. Bombardment of enemy front line on a front of 50 yards was carried out according to a prearranged scheme. The Heavy Trench Mortar cooperated	

Army Form C. 2118.

WAR DIARY
or
INTELLIGENCE SUMMARY.
(Erase heading not required.)

Place	Date	Hour	Summary of Events and Information	Remarks and references to Appendices
ARMENTIÈRES (Cont)	30/10/16 31/10/16		Enemys front line was completely demolished. 318 18pr Rounds 186 4.6" How Rounds 52 MTM bombs and 10 HTM bombs were fired. Bombardment of the day before was repeated for 5 mins.	

Newinhill
Lieutenant Colonel
Commanding 175 Brigade RFA

Vol 10

Confidential

War Diary

- of -

175th Brigade R.F.A.

From 1st to 30th Novr 1916.

Volume 4

1/5F.R.B.A

Army Form C. 2118.

WAR DIARY
INTELLIGENCE SUMMARY

RIGHT GROUP. R.A. FRANKS FORCE.
(A/152 RFA, B/175 RFA
A/175 RFA, D/175 RFA)
VOL. XI

Place	Date	Hour	Summary of Events and Information	Remarks and references to Appendices
ARMENTIERES.	1916. Nov. 3	6.0 PM	Reference Map - VIEZ MACQUART TRENCH MAP front of sheet 36. This Group co-operated with the Auckland Battalion, 2ⁿᵈ N.Z Infantry Brigade who were making a raid at C29.c.5.6.0. enemy front line West of BOX FARM. A/175, B/175 and one section of D/175 RFA fired on enemy front and support lines seven to eight hundred yards South of the point of entry, this creating a diversion. One section of D/175 RFA placed under the orders of the O.C. LEFT GROUP, ARTILLERY, FRANKS FORCE and took part in the barrage protecting the raiding party.	/
	5	2.0/6 2.30 PM and 3.30/6 4.0 PM	The 18 Pdrs of this Group fired on apparent portions of the enemy's front and support lines and the howitzer battery fired on suspected Minnenwerfer emplacements as covering fire for the Heavy and Medium Trench Mortars of the Right Group.	
	10	2.0/6 2.30 PM	This Group assisted the 2" Trench Mortars with covering fire on enemy's front line and support trenches.	
	11	5.55 AM	Hurricane bombardment by the Right Group on enemy's front line to catch working parties engaged in repairing damages in their front line trenches. 2 Rounds Gun fire by each Battery.	
	12	5.40 AM	Hurricane bombardment by this Group on enemy front and support lines for same purpose.	
		10/6 1.15 PM	A/175 and B/175 RFA fired on enemy front and support lines and D/175 fired on Minnenwerfer emplacements, 80 Rounds, as covering fire for 2" Trench Mortars of this Group who were cutting wire opposite our salient at L'EPINETTE. A/152 cut wire opposite the MUSHROOM as a blind.	

Army Form C. 2118.

175.F.A.RA

WAR DIARY
or
INTELLIGENCE SUMMARY.
Sheet 2.

(Erase heading not required.)

Instructions regarding War Diaries and Intelligence Summaries are contained in F. S. Regs., Part II. and the Staff Manual respectively. Title pages will be prepared in manuscript.

Place	Date	Hour	Summary of Events and Information	Remarks and references to Appendices
ARMENTIERES.	1916. Nov 13	2.30 to 2.40 P.M.	B/175 RFA swept the enemy's front and support lines and D/175 RFA bombarded suspected O.Ps and Minnenwerfer emplacements as covering fire to 2" Trench Mortars who were continuing wire cutting opposite our salient at L'EPINETTE. A/152 RFA again fired to cut wire opposite the MUSHROOM to divert attention.	
	14	6.20 A.M.	A "Minnen" bombardment by this Group on enemy front line to catch working party	
		3.0 to	Y/34 Trench Mortar cut wire on enemy front line in front of SPARROW'S NEST. B/175 RFA	
		3.15 PM	assisted with covering fire on support line on either side of SPARROWS NEST. D/175 RFA bombarded SPARROWS NEST, RETALIATION FARM, and LA HONGRIE FARM.	
	15	3.15 to	Y/34 Trench Mortars cut wire due WEST of SPARROWS NEST and also bombarded that place.	
		3.25 PM	B/175 RFA cut wire on enemy front N.E. of L'EPINETTE SALIENT as a diversion. A/175 RFA assisted with covering fire on enemy front and support line from SPARROWS NEST to a point due East of L'EPINETTE SALIENT and on two communication trenches opposite PORTE EGAL FM. D/175 RFA bombarded suspected O.Ps and Minnenwerfer emplacements in the vicinity of SPARROWS NEST.	
	16	1.0 to 1.15 P.M.	Y/3 + Trench Mortars cut wire due West of SPARROWS NEST ; B/175 RFA cut wire N.E. of L'EPINETTE SALIENT as a diversion. A/175 RFA assisted with covering fire on enemy front and support line from SPARROWS NEST to a point due East of L'EPINETTE SALIENT. D/175 RFA	

175 F.A.Bde. Army Form C. 2118.

WAR DIARY
or
INTELLIGENCE SUMMARY

Sheet 3.

(Erase heading not required.)

Place	Date	Hour	Summary of Events and Information	Remarks and references to Appendices
ARMENTIERES.	1916. Nov.16	1.0 to 1.15 P.M.	D/175 RFA bombarded projected O.Ps. and Minenwerfer emplacements in the vicinity of SPARROWS NEST	
	17	6.15AM	Minenwerfer bombardment by A/152, A/175 (one section) and D/175 RFA (one section) on enemy front line opposite PIGOTT'S FARM and A/175 (one section), B/175 (4 guns) and D/175 (one section) on enemy front line at the Railway salient.	
	18	5.55AM	Hurricane bombardment by this Group on enemy's front line on the North side of the Railway salient.	
		2.0 to 2.10pm	Y/34 Trench Mortars cut wire opposite the MUSHROOM and also cut wire at enemy's front line to the North East of L'EPINETTE SALIENT. A/152 RFA assisted with enemy fire on enemy's front and support lines at the RAILWAY SALIENT. B/175 RFA assisted by fire on enemy's front and support lines opposite and to NE of L'EPINETTE SALIENT. D/175 RFA fired on Minenwerfer emplacement I.11.c.95.40, SPARROWS NEST, INTACT FARM, and BRUNE RUE.	
	20	11.0 to 11.15 A.M.	Y/34 Trench Mortars cut wire at enemy's front line in front of SPARROWS NEST and also at enemy front line North East of L'EPINETTE SALIENT. D/175 RFA bombarded Dug-Outs in the vicinity of the enemy's front line in front of SPARROWS NEST (one section) and INTACT FARM and BRUNE RUE (one section). A/175 RFA swept enemy's	

WAR DIARY or INTELLIGENCE SUMMARY

Army Form C. 2118. Sheet 4.

175-F.A.Bde.

Place	Date	Hour	Summary of Events and Information	Remarks and references to Appendices
ARMENTIERES	1916. Nov 20	11.0 A / 11.15 AM	enemy's front and support lines in vicinity of SPARROW'S NEST and B/175 RFA surept- enemy's front and support lines opposite L'EPINETTE SALIENT. 6" Howitzers bombarded enemy's salient opposite North East side of L'EPINETTE SALIENT and Sap to South.	
	20/21		A raid was carried out by the 24th Battalion, Northumberland Fusiliers, 103rd Infantry Brigade. This Group with one section of the 4.5" Howitzers and one 6" Howitzer supported. Artillery fire commenced. This Group fired as follows :—	
		12.30 AM	A/175 and B/175 RFA on enemy's front line West of SPARROW'S NEST and 2 communication Trenches SOUTH WEST of SPARROW'S NEST. 180 Rounds each. D/175 RFA 120 Rounds on	
		12.45 AM	points in the vicinity of SPARROW'S NEST. Y/34 Trench Mortars on enemy's front line and wire WEST of SPARROW'S NEST, 80 bombs.	
		2.30 AM	The Batteries of this Group fired a Box Barrage behind the enemy's front line in	
		2.40 AM	vicinity of SPARROW'S NEST until covered by the Infantry that the covering party were back. The Infantry reported that the Box Barrage was excellent. They also reported that the enemy's front line trench was completely flattened and the head of the communication Trench could not be found. They had no casualties.	

WAR DIARY
or
INTELLIGENCE SUMMARY.

(Erase heading not required.)

Army Form C. 2118.

175-F.A.Bde.
Sheet 5.

Place	Date	Hour	Summary of Events and Information	Remarks and references to Appendices
ARMENTIERES	1916. Nov. 20/21		The 2nd ANZAC Cyclist Battalion were to have made a raid on enemy's front line North of the RAILWAY SALIENT at the same time but without Artillery co-operation. The enemy put up a very strong barrage in front of our wire, and the raiding party did not proceed.	
	22	5.30 AM	Hurricane Bombardment by A/152, A/175 (2 guns) B/175 (3 guns) and D/175 RFA on enemy front line in front of SPARROWS NEST and enemy front line opposite PIGOTT'S FM.	
	23	1.0 to 1.15 PM	Y/34 Trench Mortars bombarded enemy wire and parapet on SOUTH end of RAILWAY SALIENT and Communication Trench behind SPARROWS NEST, 70 Rounds. D/175 RFA bombarded SPARROWS NEST, LA FRESNELLE, A Triangle of Communication Trenche behind the RAILWAY SALIENT and Minnenwerfer emplacements in support-line opposite the MUSHROOM 40 Rounds. A/152 and B/175 RFA swept front and support-line in the vicinity.	
	26 & 27		During Tuesday the 9th Infantry Brigade A.I.F. relieved the 103rd Infantry Brigade.	
	29	6.0 AM	Hurricane Bombardment by D/175 on SPARROWS NEST and vicinity, A/175 on enemy's support line round SPARROWS NEST, B/175 on Sap opposite L'EPINETTE Salient, A/152 (2 guns) on Communication Trench from enemy's front line to SPARROWS NEST.	
		3.0 to 3.15 PM	A/152 bombarded support line opposite PIGOTTS FARM, and D/175 bombarded suspected O.Ps in NEZ MACQUART. A Minnenwerfer emplacement opposite the MUSHROOM and support line opposite PIGOTTS FARM to cover fire of 3" STOKES Mortars.	

N. Turnbull
Lieut.
Comdg 175. Brigade RFA.

Confidential

War Diary

of

175th Brigade R.F.A.

From 1st to 31st Dec. 1917

Vol XI

1916
C.T.A.

Volume 12

175th Bde RFA

Army Form C. 2118.

Instructions regarding War Diaries and Intelligence Summaries are contained in F.S. Regs., Part II. and the Staff Manual respectively. Title pages will be prepared in manuscript.

WAR DIARY
or
INTELLIGENCE SUMMARY.
RIGHT GROUP. LEFT DIVISION ARTILLERY.
(A/152. A/175; B/175; D/175.)
(Erase heading not required.)

Place	Date	Hour	Summary of Events and Information	Remarks and references to Appendices
ARMENTIERES.	1916. 2 Dec.		Reference WEZ MACQUART Trench Map. Part of Sheet 36.	
		11.30 to 11.40am	The Y/34 M.T.M. bombarded a Sap and enfilade post opposite L'EPINETTE Salient supported by covering fire from A/175 RFA on BRUNE RUE, B/175 RFA on enemy front and support line and D/175 RFA on Minnenwerfer Emplacements opposite L'EPINETTE, and his 3" Mortars bombarded on enemy front line to the North East.	
		9.30pm	Our Enemy machine gun on Eastern side of Railway Salient was fired on by A/175 and D/175 RFA	
	3rd Dec	2.0pm to 2.10pm	Y/34 M.T.M. bombarded the machine gun Emplacement fired on the previous evening. A/175 covered with fire on enemy front and support line on both sides of the Railway Salient. D/175 fired on Minnenwerfer Emplacements in its vicinity and on suspected O.Ps on WEZ MACQUART.	
	4th Dec	8.0pm and 11.0pm	Gas was Enlarged on the Left Group front. B/175 R.F.A. covered with fire on the enemy front line in front of Box and Cox Farms.	
	6th Dec	1.0pm to 1.15pm	Y/34 M.T.M. cut wire East side of SPARROWS' NEST, B/175 on enemy front and support line opposite L'EPINETTE fire in front of SPARROWS' NEST, A/152 on East Side of Railway Salient and D/175 on BRUNE RUE, SPARROWS NEST, and Minnenwerfer Emplacements in vicinity of Railway Salient	
	7th Dec	2.15pm to 2.25pm	Y/34 M.T.M. cut wire in front of SPARROWS NEST, Supported by A/175 RFA on enemy front and	

Army Form C. 2118.

WAR DIARY
or
INTELLIGENCE SUMMARY.
(Erase heading not required.)

2.

Instructions regarding War Diaries and Intelligence Summaries are contained in F. S. Regs., Part II. and the Staff Manual respectively. Title pages will be prepared in manuscript.

Place	Date	Hour	Summary of Events and Information	Remarks and references to Appendices
ARMENTIERES.	1916. 7" Dec	2.15 pm to 2.25 pm	Support line in the vicinity and D/175 R.F.A. on adjacent minenwerfer Emplacements and on machine Gun Emplacements in Enemy front line North of Railway Salient.	
	8" Dec	1.30 pm to 2.0 pm	Y/34 bombarded Enemy front line and close line of Railway Salient covered by A/175, and A/152 on Enemy front and support lines in the vicinity. D/175 on adjacent minenwerfer Emplacements and Suspected O.Ps. in WEZ MACQUART, RUELLE DE LA BLANCHE.	
	9" Dec	12.0 noon to 12.30 pm	Y/34 M.T.M. cut wire opposite the Potteau side of L'EPINETTE Salient. Y/34 H.T.M. fired on Railway Salient and Trench Mortar Emplacements to South. A/152 wire covering fire from B/175 R.F.A. on Enemy front and support line in vicinity of BRUNEROE, A/175 R.F.A. on Enemy front and support line South of Railway Salient. D/175 on Trench Mortar Emplacements at SPARROWS NEST and to N.E. thereof.	
	10" Dec	2.0 pm to 2.10 pm	Y/34 M.T.M. cut wire at Southern point of Railway Salient. A/152 R.F.A. on Enemy front and support lines opposite PIGOTTS FARM, A/175 on Enemy front and support line on Railway Salient and to the North thereof. D/175 on Junction of Communication trench in Support line opposite to MUSHROOM and on Junction of Communication trench opposite PIGOTTS FARM.	
	10/11. Dec.	1.10 am	In connection with a raid by the 34" Division on our Right Enemy machine gun Emplacements fire from opposite our front was kept down by the 9" Infantry, A.I.F., L.T.M. bombarding	

Army Form C. 2118.

WAR DIARY
or
INTELLIGENCE SUMMARY.
(Erase heading not required.)

Instructions regarding War Diaries and Intelligence Summaries are contained in F. S. Regs., Part II. and the Staff Manual respectively. Title pages will be prepared in manuscript.

Place	Date	Hour	Summary of Events and Information	Remarks and references to Appendices
ARMENTIERES	1916. Dec. 10/11	1:10 a.m.	Machine gun emplacements and trenches in the Railway Salient and Salient opposite the MUSHROOM. A/152 bombarded enemy front line and supports from the south of the Railway Salient to a point opposite PIGOTTS FARM. D/175 on a point behind enemy front line opposite Northern point of MUSHROOM and on the junction of communication trench and support line opposite southern point of MUSHROOM.	
	12 Dec	11.30 a.m. to 11.40 a.m.	Y/34 M.T.M. bombarded T Sap opposite the Northern side of L'EPINETTE Salient and front line enemy front line opposite southern side of the Salient, assisted by covering fire from A/175 on front and support line and communication trenches in the vicinity, and B/175 on the trenches in the vicinity of BRUNE RUE. D/175 on trench mortar emplacements between BRUNE RUE and SPARROWS NEST.	
		11.30 a.m. to 11.50 a.m.	V/34 H.T.M. bombarded junction of communication trenches and support line opposite Southern point of MUSHROOM, support line 100 yards to NE, and junction of trenches to S.E. A/152 R.F.A. on the front line and communication trenches in its vicinity.	
	13 Dec	2.30 pm to 2.50 pm	Y/34 M.T.M. cut wire and bombarded enemy front line in front of SPARROWS NEST. D/175 R.F.A. on trench mortar emplacements and A/175 and B/175 on front line in the vicinity.	

Army Form C. 2118.

WAR DIARY
INTELLIGENCE SUMMARY
(Erase heading not required.)

Instructions regarding War Diaries and Intelligence Summaries are contained in F. S. Regs., Part II and the Staff Manual respectively. Title pages will be prepared in manuscript.

Place	Date	Hour	Summary of Events and Information	Remarks and references to Appendices
ARMENTIERES/4.	1916. Dec 14th	5.10 pm	In co-operation with the 3rd Divisional Artillery we bombarded transport routes and	
		5.45 pm	tramlines leading up to front line from a line between LA FRESNELLE and PREMESQUES.	
	16 Dec	6.25 pm	Y/34 M.T.M. cut wire and bombarded parapet at Southern point of MUSHROOM and	
		7.50 pm	machine gun emplacement at head of communication trench opposite GRANDE PORTE	
		1.45 pm to 1.55 pm	EGAL FARM. A/152 R.F.A. on the enemy front line, support line and communication trenches opposite the MUSHROOM. A/175 R.F.A. do. do. from Railway Salient to Sparrows Nest. D/175 R.F.A. fired on trench mortar emplacements in rear of SPARROWS NEST and opposite the MUSHROOM, support line in rear of Railway Salient and O.P. at WEZ MACQUART.	
	19 Dec	2.15 p.m to 2.40 p.m	Y/34 M.T.M., and 1 Battery 3rd Australian Division M.T.M. cut wire at projecting point in enemy front line opposite N.E. side of L'EPINETTE salient. D/175 fired on trench mortar emplacements opposite the salient. A/175 with B/175 fired on the enemy front and support line and communication trenches from BRUNE RUE to SPARROWS NEST.	
	20 Dec		Visit of the Second Army Commander to all Batteries of the Group.	
	22 Dec		Inspection by the Commander-in-Chief of 34th Division.	

WAR DIARY or INTELLIGENCE SUMMARY

Army Form C. 2118.

Place	Date	Hour	Summary of Events and Information	Remarks and references to Appendices
ARMENTIERES	1916 Dec 23	2·30 pm to 2·50 pm	Y/34 M.T.M. and 3" Australian Div M.T.M. cut wire opposite the South and North of L'EPINETTE Salient respectively and bombarded parapets and delay action fuzes. Covering fire by B/175 RFA on enemy front and support line and communication trenches in front of BRUNE RUE, A/175 RFA on do do do opposite L'EPINETTE Salient D/175 RFA howitzers stood by for retaliation which was required and they fired on trench mortar emplacements in the vicinity. The 3" L.T.M. also fired on the front line opposite the Salient.	
	24 Dec	2·0 pm to 2·30 pm	Y/34 M.T.M. and 3rd Australian Div. M.T.M. bombarded support line and front line parapets from same front as before. The 18 Pdrs. by two groups fired on the same target moving Newton fuzes.	
	Night 24/25 Dec.	2·15 a.m. to 4·30 a.m.	The 9th Australian Infantry Brigade carried out a raid on the enemy trenches at the Railway Salient. This Group stood by to barrage enemy lines if called upon. The raid was unproductive. No artillery action took place.	
	26 Dec	1·15 pm to 1·30 pm	X/M.T.M. Battery A.I.F. cut wire at a point on enemy front line to S.W. of SPARROWS NEST and also opposite PIGOTTS FARM, supported by covering fire from A/152 on front line in vicinity opposite PIGOTTS FARM and on front line, communication trenches, and support line opposite the MUSHROOM. A/175 fired on trenches from the Railway Salient to 500 yards north.	

Army Form C. 2118.

WAR DIARY
of
INTELLIGENCE SUMMARY.
(Erase heading not required.)

Instructions regarding War Diaries and Intelligence Summaries are contained in F. S. Regs., Part II. and the Staff Manual respectively. Title pages will be prepared in manuscript.

No. **6.**

Place	Date	Hour	Summary of Events and Information	Remarks and references to Appendices
ARMENTIERES	1918 26 Dec	1.15 pm to 1.30 pm	B/175 RFA fired on the Enemy front line system from SPARROWS NEST to BRUNE RUE.	
	28 Dec	12.30 pm to 12.50 pm	X/M.T.M. A.I.F. bombarded Enemy Support line from South of SPARROWS NEST to 350 yards North. Y/T.M. bombarded Enemy Support line from South of SPARROWS NEST to behind Railway Salient. B/175 fired on Enemy front line system from SPARROWS NEST to point opposite L'EPINETTE Salient. A/175 RFA fired on Enemy front line system from SPARROWS NEST to Southern end of Railway Salient. D/175 RFA bombarded INTACT FARM, RETALIATION FARM and two transverse emplacements in Enemy Support line opposite the MUSHROOM.	
	29 Dec	2.10 pm to 2.20 pm 2.45 pm 2.25 pm 3.15 pm to 3.25 pm	X/M.T.M. bombarded Enemy Support line and communication trenches from SPARROWS NEST to opposite L'EPINETTE. Y/M.T.M. bombarded do. do. opposite PIGOTTS FARM and opposite GRANDE PORTE EGAL FARM. 2nd Period. X/M.T.M. cut wire opposite SPARROWS NEST and L'EPINETTE. Y/M.T.M. cut wire opposite PIGOTTS and opposite GRAND PORTE EGAL. 3rd Period: Howe batteries cut wire at the same places and bombarded the parapets giving two wire cutting and bombarding D/175 fired on Minenwerfer emplacements opposite the MUSHROOM, and opposite L'EPINETTE Salient. B/175 bombarded BRUNE RUE and INTACT FARM sunk 2 guns. 4 Grand Rounds - retaliatory fire on front line and support line between BRUNE RUE and SPARROWS NEST. A/175 bombarded SPARROWS NEST, RETALIATION FARM and Triangle in support line opposite the MUSHROOM. A/152 bombarded LA HONGRIE FARM.	

Army Form C. 2118.

WAR DIARY
or
INTELLIGENCE SUMMARY.
(Erase heading not required.)

Instructions regarding War Diaries and Intelligence Summaries are contained in F. S. Regs., Part II. and the Staff Manual respectively. Title pages will be prepared in manuscript.

Place	Date	Hour	Summary of Events and Information	Remarks and references to Appendices
	1918.			
ARMENTIERES	Night 30/31st Dec.	5.15 pm 6.10 pm 11.20 am 12.30 pm 1.5 am 1.10 am	This Group harassed the enemy's tram lines, approaches and general transport communication. A/152 RFA fired on the Roadway from western outskirts of PREMESQUES to BAS TROU and on the tram line behind the Support line opposite the MUSHROOM to a point 300 yards south. A/175 fired on the Roadway from RUELLE DE LA NOIX to the WEZ MACQUART - FRESNELLE road. B/175 fired on the Tramway running East from INTACT FARM for 600 yards and another 100 yards to the North of, and parallel with, the Tram line. B/175 also fired on the road from LA FRESNELLE running NE to the LA PREVOTE Road	

[signature]
Lt Col.
Comdy. Right Group,
1st Division Artillery

www.ingramcontent.com/pod-product-compliance
Lightning Source LLC
Chambersburg PA
CBHW081246170426
43191CB00037B/2062